Alfred's Basic Piano Library

Prep Course

FOR THE YOUNG BEGINNER

Willard A. Palmer · Morton Manus · Amanda Vick Lethco

Theory Book · Level B

INSTRUCTIONS FOR USE

1. This THEORY BOOK is designed for use with Alfred's PREP COURSE for the YOUNG BEGINNER, LESSON BOOK B, and the first assignment should be made when the student receives Lesson Book B.

2. This book is coordinated page-by-page with the LESSON BOOK. It is best to make the assignments according to the instructions in the upper right corner of each page of the THEORY BOOK, but assignments may be completed over a period of several lessons at the discretion of the teacher.

3. Many students enjoy filling in these pages so much that they will want to go beyond the assigned material. While such eagerness is commendable, it is best for the student to wait until the indicated pages in the lesson book have been covered before the corresponding material in this book is completed.

4. A number of additional concepts introduced in this book will serve to reinforce principles introduced in the LESSON BOOK. For example, it has been found that students enjoy using a pencil or baton to conduct pieces they have learned while they say or sing the words or while someone else plays the music. This activity does a great deal to promote a thorough understanding of the rhythms taught, and enhances rhythmic precision.

5. Private students are usually expected to complete theory assignments at home. This work is checked at the beginning of the next lesson. In class teaching, the theory assignments are sometimes completed at the lesson.

Layout by Linda Lusk • Illustrations by Christine Finn • Art Direction by Ted Engelbart

How to "Feel" the Rhythm!

Use with ALFRED'S PREP COURSE,
Lesson Book B, page 4.

Some words or phrases are naturally spoken in $\frac{3}{4}$ time. Others fit naturally in $\frac{4}{4}$ time.

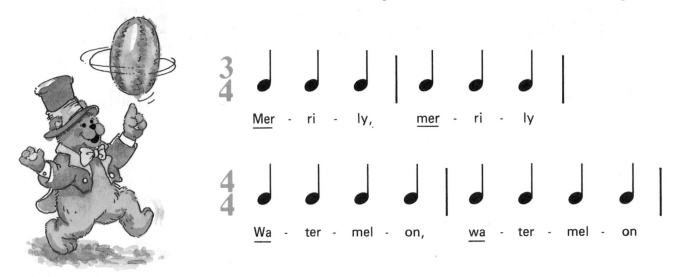

1. Say the first line below several times, clapping once for each note. Decide whether the line fits best in $\frac{3}{4}$ time or $\frac{4}{4}$ time. Add the time signature and bar lines. Do the same with each line.

You Can Direct Music!

These patterns are used by band leaders and symphony conductors.

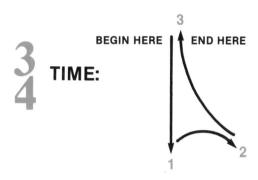

TIME: BEGIN HERE | END HERE

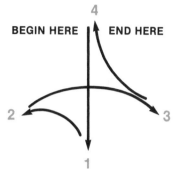

TIME: BEGIN HERE | END HERE

2. Trace these $\frac{3}{4}$ patterns with a pencil.

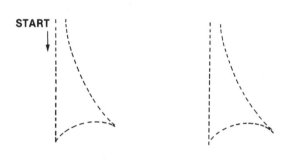

START

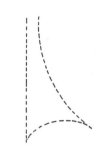

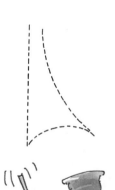

3. Using your pencil as a baton, make the $\frac{3}{4}$ pattern in the air.

4. Conduct each line of $\frac{3}{4}$ time on page 2, saying the words aloud.

5. Trace these $\frac{4}{4}$ patterns with a pencil.

START

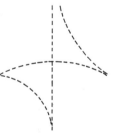

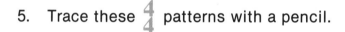

6. Using your pencil as a baton, make the $\frac{4}{4}$ pattern in the air.

7. Conduct each line of $\frac{4}{4}$ time on page 2, saying the words aloud.

Notice that the 1st beat of each measure is always a **DOWN BEAT** and the last beat of each measure is always an **UP BEAT**. This is true in any time signature!

Use with page 5.

Legato Playing

LEGATO means SMOOTHLY CONNECTED.

Slurs are curved lines over or under the notes. They tell us to PLAY LEGATO.

SLURS often divide the
music into PHRASES.   A PHRASE is a musical thought or sentence.

Clouds

1. Draw slurs connecting the first note and last note of each pair of measures.

2. Play the piece. Connect the notes of each phrase. Lift the hand at the end of each phrase.

Moderately slow

3. Conduct *CLOUDS* while you say or sing the words.

Right Side Up & Upside Down!

In some pieces you play, a tune is played "RIGHT SIDE UP" and "UPSIDE DOWN."

Notice what happens in these four measures.

1. Play the melody as you sing the words.

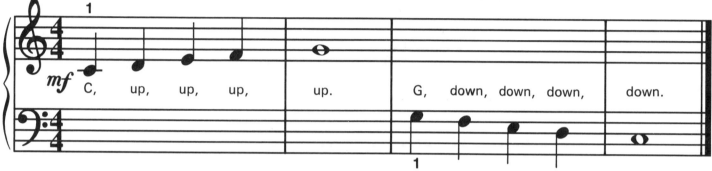

mf   C,   up,   up,   up,   up.   G,   down, down, down,   down.

Sometimes, instead of moving up or down to another line or space, notes will REPEAT on the SAME line or space. When the pattern is turned upside down, these repetitions are also made.

2. In the 3rd & 4th measures below, write the melody of the 1st & 2nd measures, UPSIDE DOWN.

3. In the 7th & 8th measures, write the melody of the 5th & 6th measures, UPSIDE DOWN.

4. Play and sing or say the words.

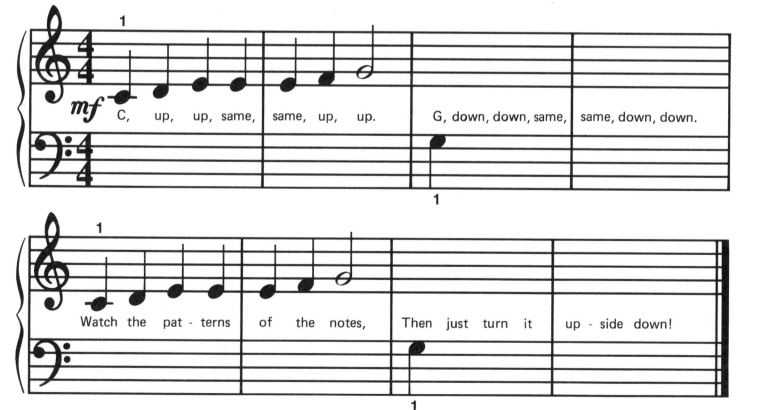

mf   C,   up,   up,   same,   same, up,   up.   G, down, down, same,   same, down, down.

Watch the pat - terns   of   the notes,   Then just turn it   up - side down!

5. Conduct the music on this page while you say or sing the words.

6

Use with pages 7 & 8.

Measuring 2nds

The distance from any white key to
the next white key, up or down, is called a **2nd.**

2nds are written LINE-SPACE or SPACE-LINE:

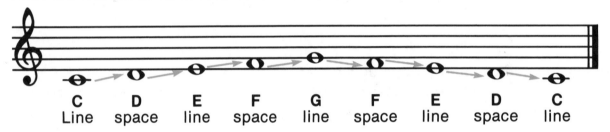

C	D	E	F	G	F	E	D	C
Line	space	line	space	line	space	line	space	line

1. In the music below, trace the arrows between the notes while saying the words
   above the notes ("Up a 2nd," etc.).

2. Write the note name under each note, then play, saying "Up a 2nd," etc.

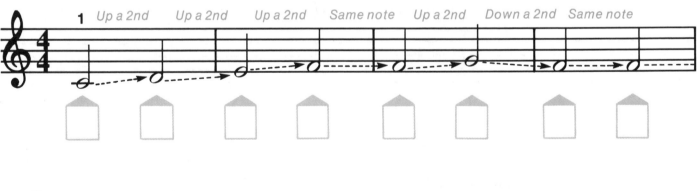

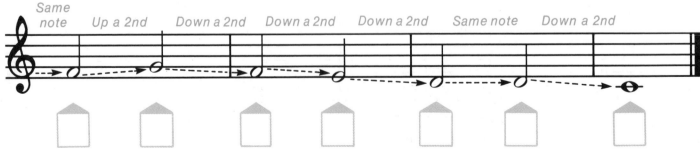

3. In the music below, trace the arrows between the notes while saying "Down a 2nd," etc.

4. Write the note name under each note, then play, saying "Down a 2nd," etc.

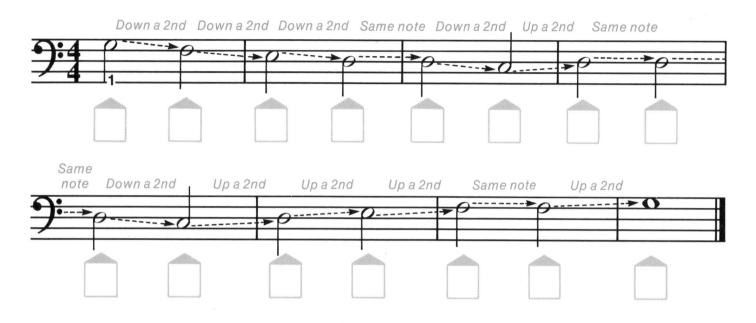

5. In each blank measure below, write a dotted half note that is a 2nd HIGHER
than the note in the measure just before it.

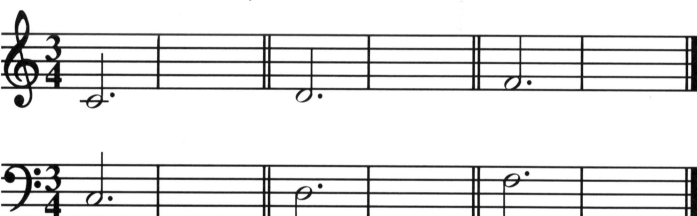

6. In each blank measure below, write a dotted half note that is a 2nd LOWER
than the note in the measure just before it.

8

Use with page 9.

Tied Notes

When notes on the SAME LINE or SAME SPACE are joined by a curved line,
we call them TIED NOTES.

The key is held down for the COMBINED VALUES OF BOTH NOTES.

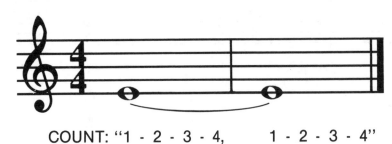

COUNT: "1 - 2 - 3 - 4,   1 - 2 - 3 - 4"

1. How long would you hold the key down for each pair of tied notes?
    Write the TOTAL number of counts for each pair of tied notes in the boxes below.

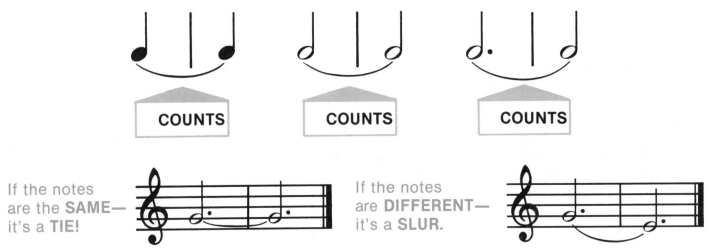

| COUNTS | COUNTS | COUNTS |

If the notes
are the **SAME**—
it's a **TIE!**

If the notes
are **DIFFERENT**—
it's a **SLUR.**

Hold the notes, without repeating!   Connect the notes, LEGATO!

TIES & SLURS

2. Write a **T** (for tie) or **S** (for slur) in the box under each pair of notes, as shown in the first box:

My Magic Balloon

1. Complete the time signatures.
2. Add the missing bar lines. Draw a double bar line at the end.
3. Add the slurs by tracing over the dotted lines.
4. Play.

Happily

Come with me, and a - way we'll fly,

Oh, so high, in the sky!

Like the clouds we'll go sail - ing by,

In my mag - ic bal - loon!

5. Conduct *MY MAGIC BALLOON* while you say or sing the words.

Measuring 3rds

Use with page 10.

When you skip a white key, the interval is a **3rd.**

3rds are written LINE-LINE or SPACE-SPACE.

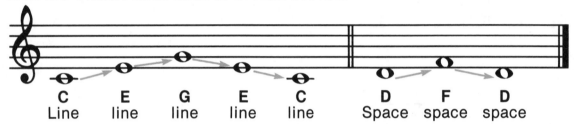

C	E	G	E	C	D	F	D
Line	line	line	line	line	Space	space	space

1. In the music below, trace the arrows between the notes while saying "Up a 3rd, same note," etc.
2. Write the note name under each note, then play, saying "Up a 3rd," etc.

Up a 3rd   Same note   Up a 3rd   Same note   Down a 3rd   Down a 3rd

Up a 3rd   Same note   Up a 3rd   Down a 3rd   Same note   Down a 3rd

3. Write the names on the keys, going up the keyboard in 3rds.

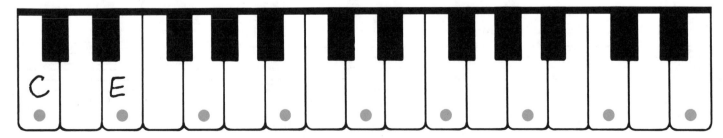

2nds & 3rds

1. Write 2 (for 2nd) or 3 (for 3rd) in the box below each pair of keys, as shown in the first box.

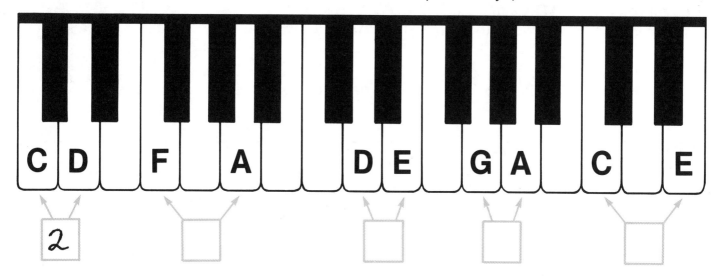

2. Write the name of the interval (2 or 3) in the box below each pair of notes, as shown in the first box.

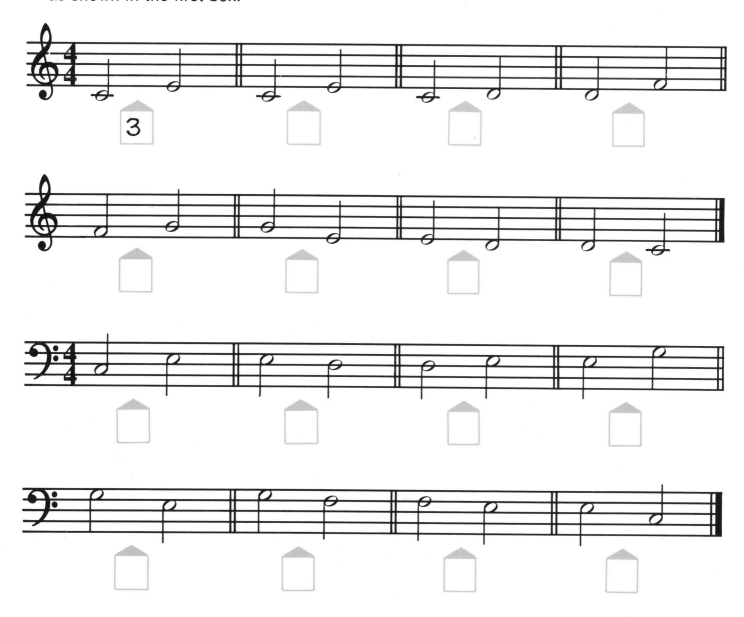

Melodic Intervals

Use with pages 14 & 15.

Notes played **SEPARATELY** make a **MELODY**.
We call the intervals between these notes **MELODIC INTERVALS.**

1. Play these MELODIC 2nds & 3rds. Say the name of each interval as you play.

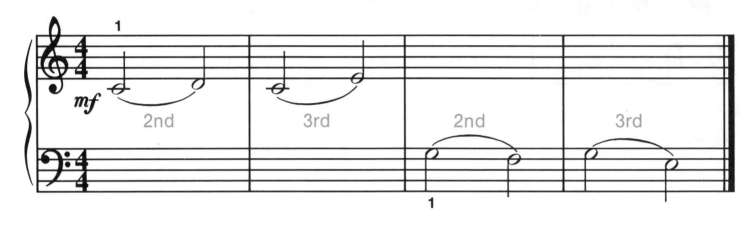

REMEMBER: 2nds go from a LINE to the very next SPACE,
or from a SPACE to the very next LINE.

3rds go from a LINE to the very next LINE,
or from a SPACE to the very next SPACE.

2. After each note, add another HALF NOTE making a melodic interval ABOVE the given note.

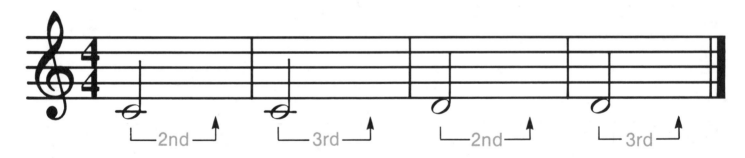

3. After each note, add another HALF NOTE making a melodic interval BELOW the given note.

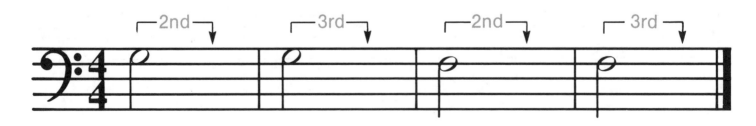

Harmonic Intervals

Notes played **TOGETHER** make **HARMONY.**
We call the intervals between these notes **HARMONIC INTERVALS.**

1. Play these HARMONIC **2nds** & **3rds.** Say the name of each interval as you play.

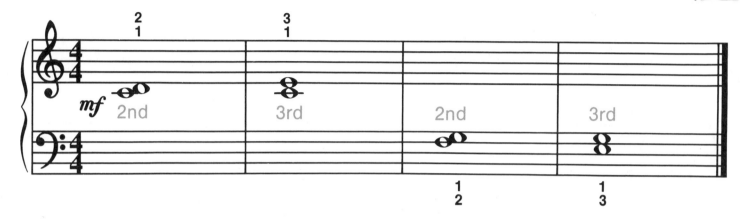

IMPORTANT! The notes of **HARMONIC 2nds** are written SIDE-BY-SIDE, touching:
The lower note is written to the left.

The notes of **HARMONIC 3rds** are written ONE ABOVE THE OTHER:

2. Above each note, add another WHOLE NOTE making a harmonic interval ABOVE the given note.

2nd   3rd   2nd   3rd

3. Below each note, add another WHOLE NOTE making a harmonic interval BELOW the given note.

2nd   3rd   2nd   3rd

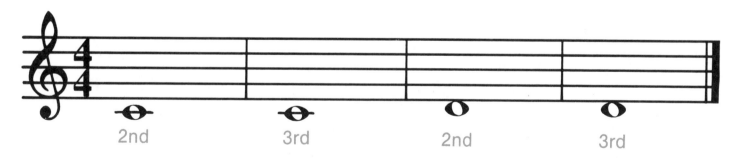

Use with page 16.

Quarter Rests

RESTS are signs of SILENCE.

 This is a **QUARTER REST.**
It means SILENCE FOR THE VALUE
OF A QUARTER NOTE.

COUNT "1" OR "QUARTER"
FOR EACH QUARTER REST!

1. Trace the 2nd quarter rest, then draw 5 more.

2. Under each note or rest in the following line of music, write the number of counts it receives.
3. Play and count.

Fish Talk

Moderately slow

1. When my gold - fish   talks to   me,   he   says, "_____."
2. He's as qui - et   as   can   be,   he   says, "_____."

4. Play *FISH TALK* and COUNT.
5. Play and sing or say the words. Make a fish face with your mouth for each rest, if you wish.
6. Conduct *FISH TALK* while you say or sing the words.
   Say "REST" for each quarter rest.

Whole Rests

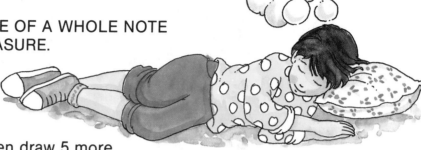

This is a **WHOLE REST.**

It means SILENCE FOR THE VALUE OF A WHOLE NOTE
or any WHOLE MEASURE.

1. Fill in the 2nd WHOLE REST, then draw 5 more.
The WHOLE REST hangs down from the 4th line of the staff.

2. In SILENT MARCH and SILENT WALTZ, add a WHOLE REST to each measure
that doesn't have one.

Silent March

Moderately fast

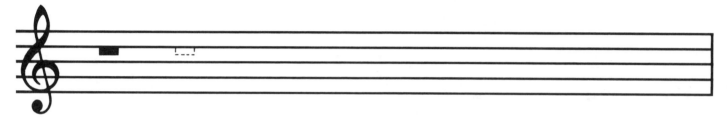

p

Silent Waltz

Moderately fast

p

3. Play SILENT MARCH with LH and count.
4. Play SILENT WALTZ with RH and count.

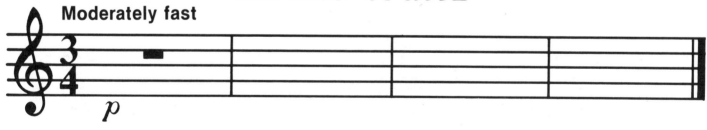

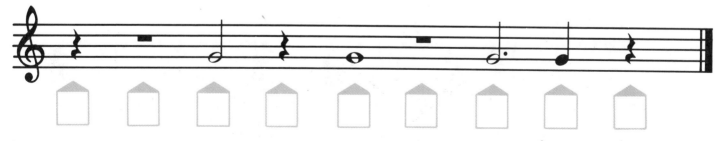

5. Below each rest or note write the number of counts it receives in 4/4 time.

16

Measuring 4ths

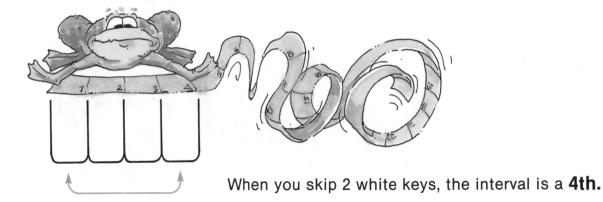

When you skip 2 white keys, the interval is a **4th.**

4ths are written LINE-SPACE or SPACE-LINE.

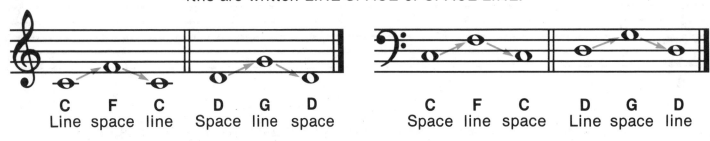

1. In the music below, trace the arrows between the notes while saying the words above the notes.
2. Write the name under each note, then play, saying "Up a 4th," etc.

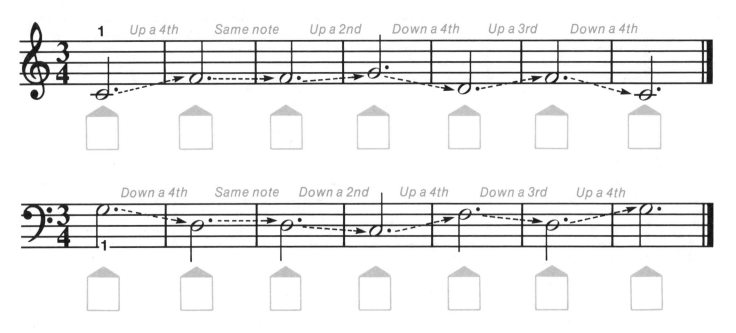

3. Write the names on the keys, going up the keyboard in 4ths.

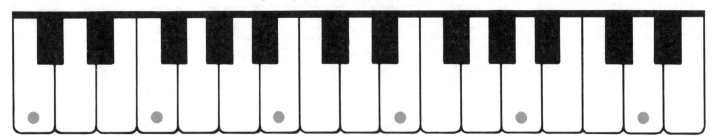

2nds, 3rds & 4ths

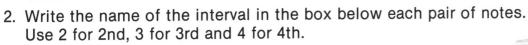

1. The intervals in the two lines below are *melodic* or *harmonic* intervals.
   Underline the correct word.
2. Write the name of the interval in the box below each pair of notes.
   Use 2 for 2nd, 3 for 3rd and 4 for 4th.

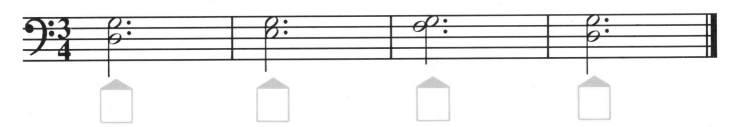

3. The intervals in the two lines below are *melodic* or *harmonic* intervals.
   Underline the correct word.
4. Write the name of each interval in the box below it.
   Use 2 for 2nd, 3 for 3rd and 4 for 4th.

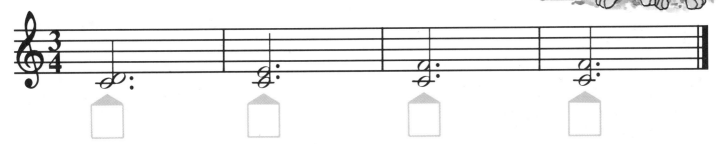

5. In each measure below, write another whole note to make the indicated HARMONIC interval.

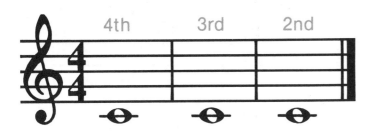

Reviewing Rests

Use with page 23.

RESTS ARE SIGNS OF SILENCE

QUARTER REST: 𝄽   means silence for the value of a quarter note.

HALF REST: ▬   means silence for the value of a half note.

WHOLE REST: ▬   means silence for the value of a whole note or for any whole measure.

1. Trace the 2nd QUARTER REST, then draw 5 more.

2. Fill in the 2nd HALF REST, then draw 5 more.
   The HALF REST sits on the 3rd line of the staff!

3. Fill in the 2nd WHOLE REST, then draw 5 more. The whole rest hangs down from the 4th line!

4. Name these rests. Use Q for QUARTER, H for HALF, and W for WHOLE.

5. In the square below each rest, write the number of counts it receives in $\frac{4}{4}$ time.

Quiet, Please!

This piece should be very easy to play.
The problem is that there is a mistake in every measure!

1. Correct each mistake by writing exactly ONE rest
   in the RH or LH of each measure that
   does not have enough counts.

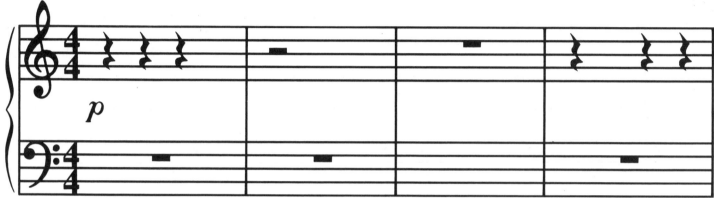

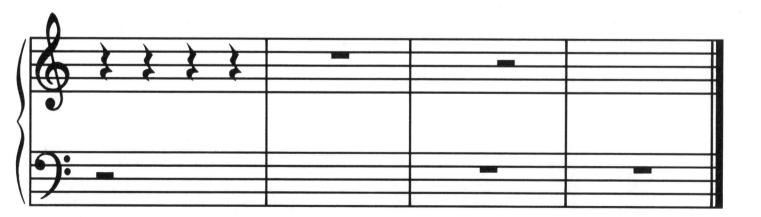

2. Direct *QUIET, PLEASE!* Say "REST" for each quarter rest, "HALF REST" for each half rest,
   and "WHOLE REST, FOUR BEATS" for each whole rest.

Measuring 5ths

Use with page 26.

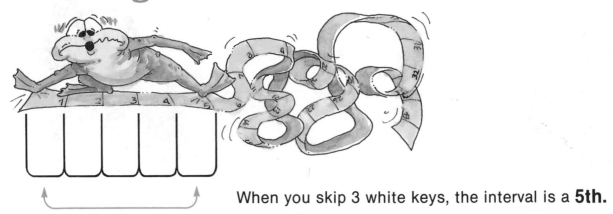

When you skip 3 white keys, the interval is a **5th.**

5ths are written LINE-LINE or SPACE-SPACE.

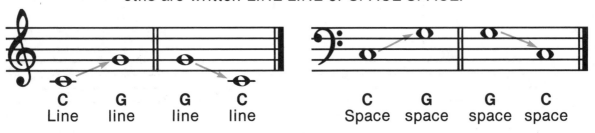

| **C** | **G** | **G** | **C** | | **C** | **G** | **G** | **C** |
| Line | line | line | line | | Space | space | space | space |

1. In the music below, trace the arrows between the notes while saying the words above the notes.

2. Write the name under each note, then play, saying "Up a 5th," etc.

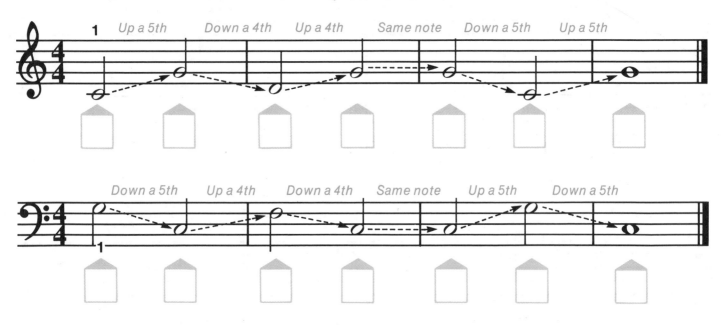

3. Write the names on the keys, going up the keyboard in 5ths.

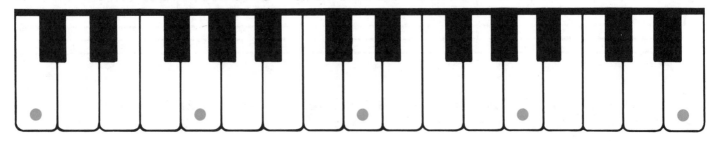

Use with pages 27–29.

2nds, 3rds, 4ths & 5ths

1. The intervals in the two lines below are *melodic* or *harmonic* intervals.
   Underline the correct word.
2. Write the name of the interval in the box below each pair of notes.
   Use 2 for 2nd, etc.

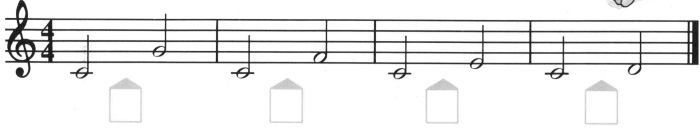

3. The intervals in the next two lines are *melodic* or *harmonic* intervals.
   Underline the correct word.
4. Write the name of each interval in the box below it. Use 2 for 2nd, etc.

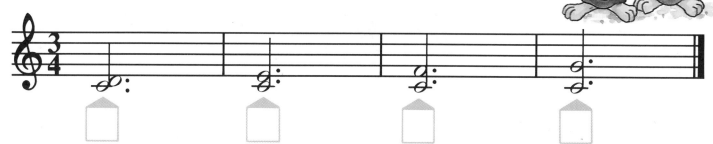

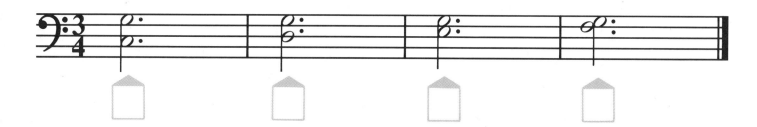

5. In each measure below, write another whole note to make the indicated HARMONIC interval.

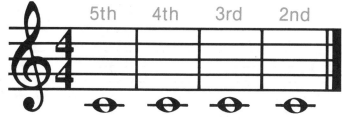

Playing in G Position

Use with page 30.

The position shown below, with each hand playing G A B C D, is called G POSITION.

1. Draw a line from each note, straight up to the key it indicates.
2. Add the correct LH finger numbers under the notes in the BASS CLEF.
3. Add the correct RH finger numbers over the notes in the TREBLE CLEF.

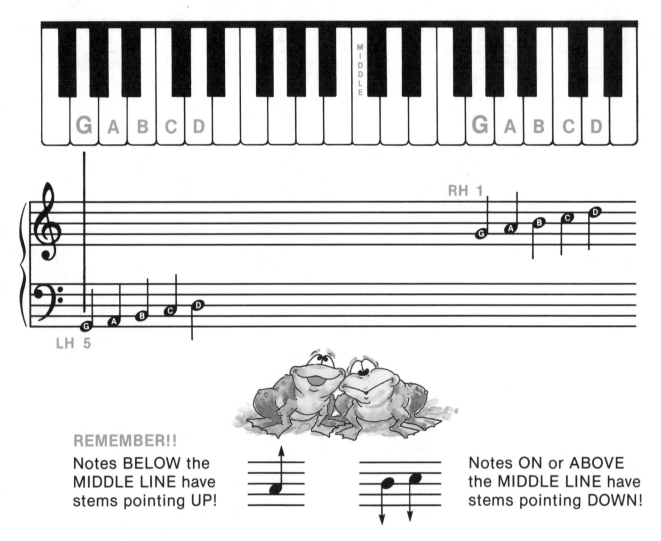

REMEMBER!!
Notes BELOW the MIDDLE LINE have stems pointing UP!

Notes ON or ABOVE the MIDDLE LINE have stems pointing DOWN!

4. Write the LH notes in the BASS staff, under the boxes. Use QUARTER NOTES.
    Turn the stems of G A B & C **UP.** Turn the stem of D **DOWN.**

5. Write the RH notes in the TREBLE staff, over the boxes. Use QUARTER NOTES.
    Turn the stems of G & A **UP.** Turn the stems of B C & D **DOWN.**

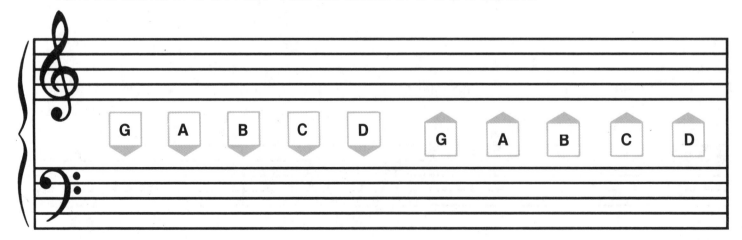

The Band-Leader

1. Write the names of the notes in the boxes.   2. Play.

Moderately fast, like a march

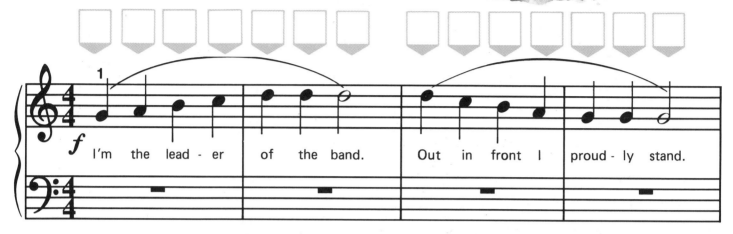

I'm the lead - er of the band.   Out in front I   proud - ly stand.

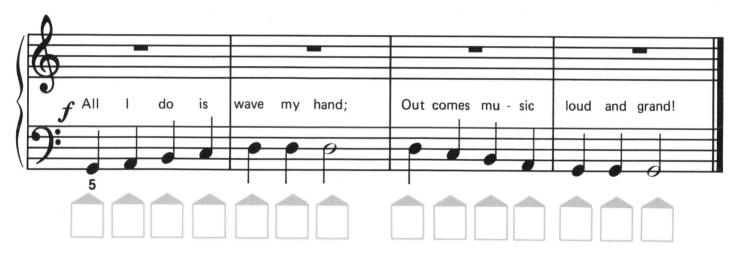

All I do is   wave my hand;   Out comes mu - sic   loud and grand!

3. Conduct *THE BAND LEADER* while you say or sing the words.

Spelling Game

4. Write the name of each note in the square below it to spell familiar words.

Use with pages 32 & 33.

Melodic Intervals in G Position

1. Write the names of the notes in the boxes above the staffs.
2. Write the names of the intervals in the boxes below the staffs. Use 2 for 2nd, etc.

Harmonic Intervals in G Position

3. Write the names of the notes in the boxes above the staffs. Write the name of the lower note in the lower box, and the name of the higher note in the higher box.
4. Write the names of the intervals in the boxes below the staffs. Use 2 for 2nd, etc.

A Star Performance!

Using a ruler or other straight edge, draw a line from the dot nearest each interval to the dot nearest its correct name. If 2 intervals have the same name, draw 2 lines.

If you draw the lines correctly, a large STAR will appear on the page.

4th •

2nd
•

3rd

5th •  •

Use with page 34.

Sharps

The **SHARP SIGN** ♯ before a note means play the next key to the right, whether black or white.

1. Make some SHARP SIGNS:

First, draw the two vertical lines. Then, add the heavy slanting lines.

Draw 4 sharp signs here.

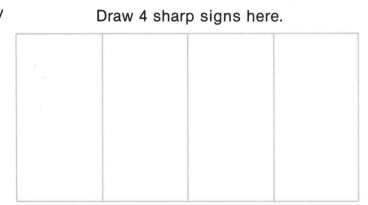

2. Write the names of the ♯ keys in the boxes:

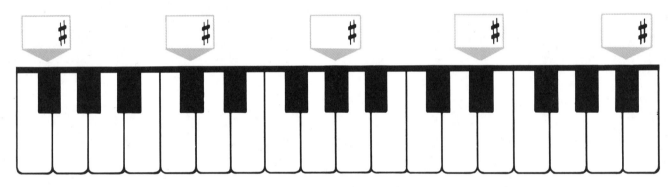

3. Change each of the notes on the staffs below to a sharp note. Play each with RH 3 or LH 3. Say the name of each note ("G sharp," etc.) as you play.

When writing sharp signs, be sure the CENTER of the sign is on the line or space of the note to be sharped:

Place the sharp BEFORE the note:

More Sharps

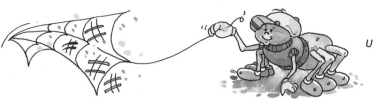

When a sharp sign appears before a note, it applies to that note for the rest of the measure.

1. Draw a circle around each note that is played as a sharp.
2. Play several times. Play slowly at first, then a little faster.

The Merry-Go-Round

3. Play. Notice that C♯ and D
   are played together with LH 2 & 1
   in the 1st, 2nd, 5th and 6th measures.

Moderately slow

Use with page 36.

Flats

The **FLAT SIGN** ♭ before a note means play the next key to the left, whether black or white.

1. Make some FLAT SIGNS:

First, draw one vertical line.

Then add the heavier curved line.

Draw 4 flat signs here.

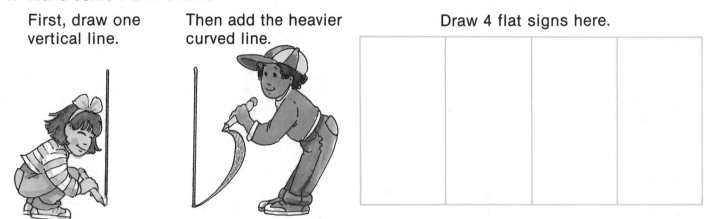

2. Write the names of the ♭ keys in the boxes.

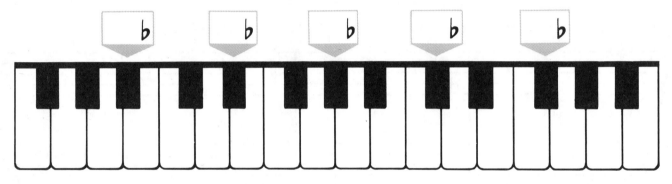

3. Change each of the notes on the staffs below to a flat note. Play each with RH 3 or LH 3. Say the name of each note ("B flat," etc.) as you play.

Be sure to CENTER the flat sign on the line or space of the note to be flatted:

Place the flat BEFORE the note:

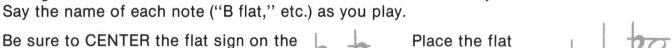

4. Can you read this motto?

ALWAYS  AND YOU'LL NEVER  !

More Flats

When a flat sign appears before a note, it applies to that note for the rest of the measure.

1. Draw a circle around each note that is played as a flat.
2. Play several times. Play slowly at first, then a little faster.

Bass Combo

3. Add a FLAT SIGN before every B in this piece.
4. Play with LH.

Moderately fast

Use with page 38.

Mystery Puzzle:
WHO ATE THE COOKIES?
(Interval Review)

Someone ate the cookies! All of them! And they were hidden in a

 under the  !

To find who was caught eating the cookies, follow these clues:

1. Start on any F. Go UP a 2nd,
   then DOWN a 5th,
   then UP a 4th,
   then DOWN a 3rd.

   What key did you end on? Write the name of the key in the
   1st square at the bottom of this page.

2. Start on any B. Go DOWN a 3rd,
   then UP a 4th,
   then DOWN a 5th
   then UP a 2nd,
   then UP a 5th,
   then DOWN a 4th.

   Write the name of the key you ended on in the 2nd square
   at the bottom of this page.

3. Start on any E. Go UP a 4th,
   then DOWN a 3rd,
   then UP a 5th,
   then DOWN a 4th,
   then DOWN a 5th,
   then UP a 2nd.

   Write the name of the key you ended on in the 3rd square
   at the bottom of this page.

Have you solved the mystery?

WHO ATE THE COOKIES?

ANSWER:

Reviewing C Position & G Position

1. Add a stem to each of these notes.

   If the note-head is below the middle line of the staff, turn the stem UP.

   If the note-head is on or above the middle line of the staff, turn the stem DOWN.

2. Write the names of the notes in the boxes.

3. In the music below, write the names of the notes in the boxes.
4. Play. Watch for changes in hand positions.

5. Direct the above two lines of music, saying the note names aloud.
   For each quarter rest, say "REST."

Staccato Playing

Use with page 40.

STACCATO means SEPARATED or DETACHED.
To play STACCATO, release the key the instant you play it.

Staccato is indicated by a DOT over ♩ or under ♩ the note.

Dueling Staccatos

1. Add a STACCATO DOT to each of the following notes. If the note stem points DOWN, put the dot OVER the note. If the stem points UP, put the dot UNDER the note.
2. Play. Watch for changes in hand positions.

Moderately

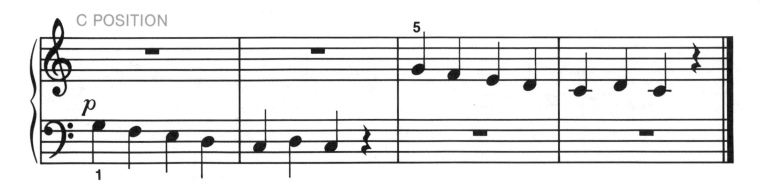

3. Direct *DUELING STACCATOS,* saying the names of the notes aloud. For each quarter rest, say "REST."

Staccato is the Opposite of Legato!

STACCATO notes are SEPARATED or DETACHED.
LEGATO notes are SMOOTHLY CONNECTED.

1. Write **S** under each staccato note below.   2. Write **L** under each legato note below.

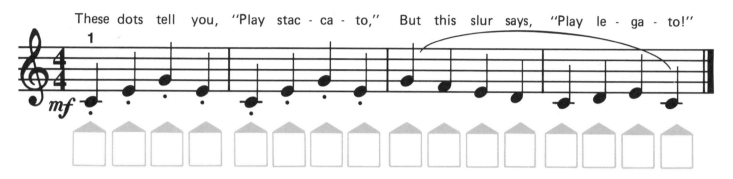

3. Play the above. Carefully observe the staccato and legato signs.

Sometimes LEGATO notes are connected smoothly to a STACCATO note. In such a case only the LAST note is played staccato, while the rest are played legato:

Indian Voices

(G POSITION)

4. Write **L** under each legato note.   5. Write **S** under each staccato note.

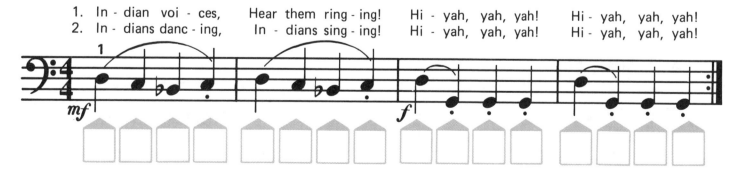

6. Play *INDIAN VOICES*. Observe everything.

Use with page 42.

New Dynamics

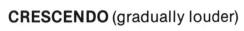

CRESCENDO (gradually louder)

DIMINUENDO (gradually softer)

1. Under the treble staff below, add a sign between the 1st p & the f meaning *gradually louder.*

2. Add a sign between the 2nd f & the p meaning *gradually softer.*

3. Study the music. Note the HAND POSITION.
   Notice which note is made FLAT each time it occurs.

4. Play with RH. Carefully observe the phrasing and dynamics!

Moderately slow

5. Between the music and the words below, add a crescendo and a diminuendo to suit the words.

6. Study the music. Note the HAND POSITION.
   Notice which note is made SHARP each time it occurs.

7. Play with LH. Carefully observe the phrasing and dynamics!

Moderately slow

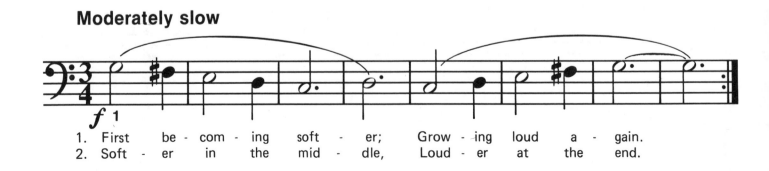

Reviewing Dynamic Signs

Draw lines connecting the dots on the matching boxes.

Score 20 for each pair of boxes correctly connected.

PERFECT SCORE = 120   YOUR SCORE: _____

Use with page 43.

Reviewing Note Values & Rests

Draw lines connecting the dots on the matching boxes.

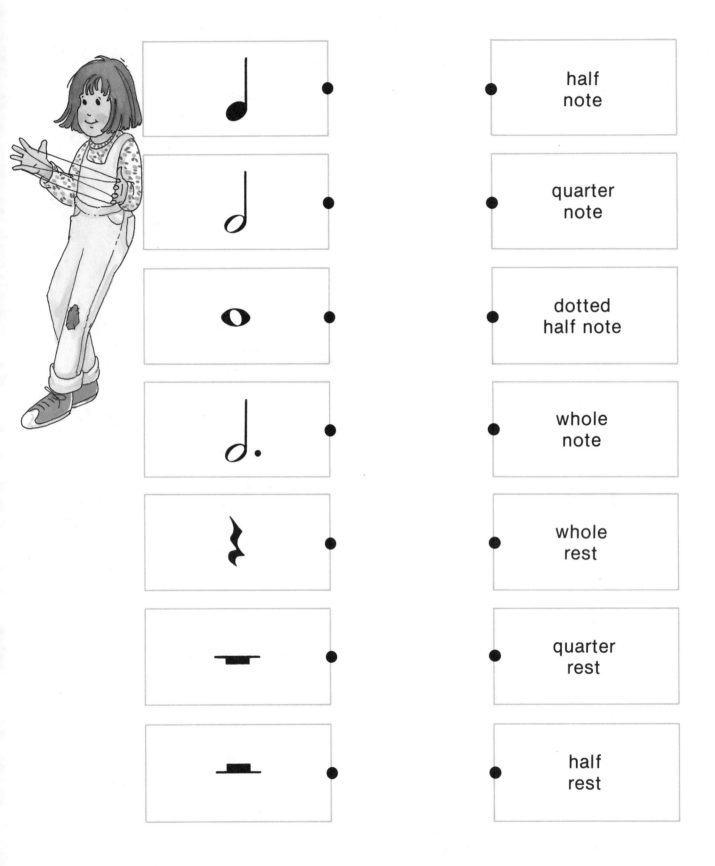

Score 20 for each pair of boxes correctly connected.

PERFECT SCORE = 140

YOUR SCORE: _____

Recognizing Hand Positions

In LEVEL B you have played in two five-finger positions, C POSITION & G POSITION.
It is very easy to instantly recognize these positions on the bass and treble staffs.
You can identify the position of the RH or LH if you know just ONE NOTE and
ONE FINGER NUMBER for each hand in each position.

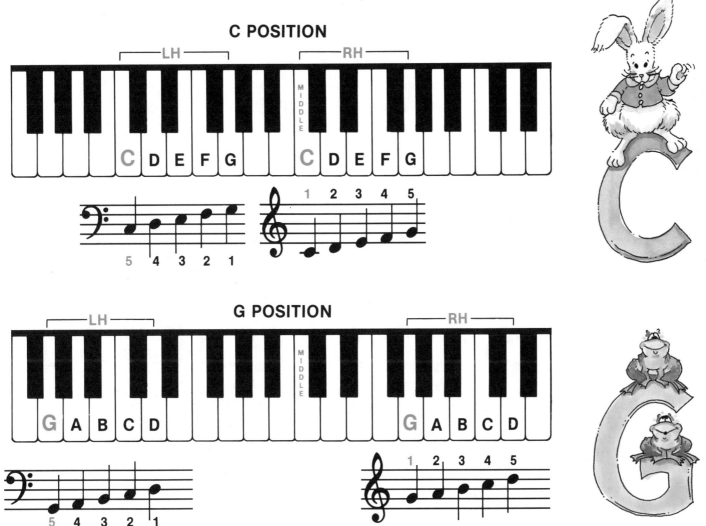

1. Write the name of the five-finger position in the box following each of these examples:

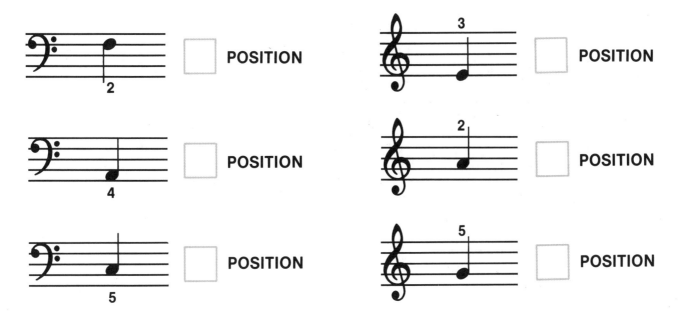

38

TRUE-FALSE QUIZ No. 1

Use with pages 44 & 45.

In the boxes, write T for TRUE, F for FALSE.

1. **3/4** means 3 beats in a measure. A quarter note gets one beat.

2. **4/4** means 4 beats in each measure. A half note gets one beat.

3. This is a DOTTED HALF NOTE.

4. This is a STACCATO HALF NOTE.

5. This is a DOTTED HALF NOTE.

6. This is a HALF REST.

7. This is a WHOLE REST.

8. This is a QUARTER REST.

9. This is a MELODIC 2nd.

10. This is a HARMONIC 5th.

Score 10 points for each correct answer.
PERFECT SCORE = 100.

YOUR SCORE: _____

TRUE-FALSE QUIZ No. 2

In the boxes, write T for TRUE, F for FALSE.

1. *mf* means much faster.

2. *p* means soft.

3. ◁——————▷ means gradually slower.

4. ◁——————▷ means gradually louder.

5. A SHARP SIGN (♯) means play the next key to the left.

6. A FLAT SIGN (♭) means play the next key to the left.

7. These notes are TIED.

8. These notes are SLURRED.

9. *f-p* means fast the first time, slow the second time.

10. LEGATO means smoothly connected.

Score 10 points for each correct answer.
PERFECT SCORE = 100.   YOUR SCORE: _____

Use with pages 46 & 47.

Things I Have Learned About Music

Use this page to list or draw all the different signs and other things you have learned about music.

You can include note values, rest values, dynamic signs, intervals, clefs, time signatures, and many other things you can think of.

Try to do this first without looking back through this book or the Lesson Book.

18 different items is a good score.

22 is VERY GOOD.

More than 22 is OUTSTANDING!

How many did you remember?   TOTAL = _____